Christian Witness

Parbar Study Aids: 1

Christian Witness

to the gospel of peace
in a culture of conflict

RS Robertson

Parbar Study Aids: 1

Parbar Publishing

Contents

Preface

This 11,000 word academic dissertation is offered to students and thinkers who wish to consider the subject of peaceable Christian witness in an academic way. It was submitted to the University of Edinburgh's School (faculty) of Divinity in 2008 as part of the author's final examinations – for which RS Robertson was awarded a first class honours degree.

In this edition:

~ Footnotes are italicised and included in the text within square brackets.

~ Latin and German words are italicised.

~ Greek characters are transliterated.

David Robertson; Parbar Publishing

Introduction

In the last words Jesus spoke to his followers, recorded in the book of Acts, he told them quite unequivocally that they would be his witnesses (Acts 1:8). The verbal sense of witnessing, at certain times in certain places, is not given here, and there is no notion of the follower choosing on particular occasions to witness. The disciples are told that they simply are witnesses. Yet for such a clear statement, the reality of being a witness seems to bear a paradox. A Christian witnesses to Jesus Christ and his kingdom, and that kingdom is a kingdom of peace, however, this witness is not always going to be met with peace – a fact which has proven true in different ways in different social contexts, and which remains apparent in the current cultural climate. Whilst Christians in the twenty-first century West do not face the kind of persecution brought against the early church or Christians living in more hostile countries at present, the society of the twenty-first century West does not unanimously believe that God is the one source of truth, or that the Church has sole authoritative access to that truth. Indeed, identifying one

Church can prove a most complicated task on its own – particularly for those who do not profess membership of it. Neither will every individual attest to the reality of the kingdom of heaven, or agree that there is an authoritative ethic that should be adhered to in this life as an anticipation of the way of life in that kingdom. Yet, the Christian bears witness to the fact that there is one true God, and that there is one way, truth, and life, and so witness is fundamentally in conflict with the worldview of many of those to whom witness is borne.

In this dissertation it will be argued that peace is an essential part of the object of Christian witness, but that peace must be understood in terms of what has been revealed in Jesus Christ; not as compromise, security, or the elimination of difference. Peace must also be conceived of as a real possibility for the present, and not only as something to be eschatologically realised. It will also be proposed that there is an 'extraordinary' quality intrinsic to the Christian life which inevitably leads to conflict with the world, (see Bonhoeffer's analysis of this term in Chapter Four of this dissertation). This conflict is not to be diminished by any of these un-Christological understandings of peace, but neither should the Christian deliberately seek conflict in the name of declaring the uniqueness of Christianity. Christianity is a movement of peace which reflects the nature of the God it worships, and it is in the uncompromising living-out of peace, in the form of unconditional love, that sets the Christian witness in such stark contrast to the world. The task of this dissertation is to find a model of witness that will hold these elements of harmony and dissonance with the world in tension, and after discussing several possible solutions, this discussion will finally turn to the work of Dietrich Bonhoeffer, who it will be suggested, describes a model of witness that does just this.

The preliminary task of this essay will be to identify and critically assess three possible understandings of the form of witness, which will be called 'self-effacing', 'symbolic', and 'significant'. Using the principles established in that assessment, this investigation will proceed with an examination of three models for the practise of witness, which for present purposes will be classified as 'peaceable', 'differential', and 'peaceably different'. The ideas of what it is to be a witness, and what it is to respond to opposition to that witness as a Christian, have been treated in various ways by many theologians. But the main texts considered in chapters two to four of this dissertation have proved to be particularly insightful because their authors lived in contexts where the question of witness was crucial, because the form of opposition, though different for each, was clear and often overtly hostile. Various thinkers will be introduced to unpack the proposed forms and models of witness, but it should be noted that this is done, not with the intention of giving particular labels to particular theologians or of placing their theological ideas within definitive categories, but in order that the implications of their ideas can serve as signposts by which a path can be navigated towards an understanding of what it is to be a Christian witness.

The Form of Witness

The first task, then, is to clarify what is formally meant by witness by examining three possibilities, the first of which to be considered will be the 'self-effacing' form. This form of witness can be defined as witness that points solely beyond itself; witness that functions as an instrument through which another can encounter God. This idea is elucidated by considering Oliver O'Donovan's understanding that the remit of the witness is to "bring the observer to equality of perspective with the witness himself" [*O'Donovan, Oliver, Resurrection and Moral Order: An Outline for Evangelical Ethics, Leicester, Inter-Varsity, 1986, p146*]. Giving the example of Socrates, O'Donovan shows how although Socrates' death bears witness to the virtues of integrity and courage, and although it took a man like Socrates to bear such a witness, it is yet possible that another person could live and die in such a way as to witness to the same thing, and so "the authority of a witness is interchangeable in principle" [*Ibid, p146*]. The point is that: although Socrates exemplified certain virtues, this in itself does not attest to the goodness of those virtues, but rather his dying for their sake testified to their goodness independent of his own moral example. Thereby more than being interchangeable, "the moral authority of a particular witness is in principle self-effacing; it aims to open the observer's eyes to the moral order and so make itself, as mediator, redundant" [*Ibid, p146*]. Conversely, Jesus' witness had a wholly unique character, for in this particular case "the witness and the object of the witness are one" [*Ibid, p147*]. What this means for the follower of Jesus, however, is that the only way in which his witness can be authoritative is the witnesses "non-identity" [*Ibid, p147*] with the object of the witness to be entirely 'self-effacing'. In one sense, this form of witness complies with a kind of Lutheran anthropology, which holds that humans are irrevocably sinners, and that the righteousness of the believer is in fact the 'alien' righteousness of Christ, imputed rather than infused to him. [*See: Luther, Martin, Luther's Works, Vol.25; Lectures on Romans, ed. Hilton C. Oswald, Saint Louis, Concordia Publishing House, 1972, especially pp206, 211*]. As a sinner, the believer must direct all attention to the proper object of their witness, from whom they receive the grace by which they are justified. This model of witness, though, must be held in tension with St. Paul's testimony: "I no longer live, but Christ lives in me" (Galatians 2:20) which indicates that if Christ's presence in the believer is in some sense a reality, then the witness *really* embodies in the witness that to which they bear witness, and so can faithfully bear witness to God – not by being totally self-effacing but by pointing to themself as a living sign of God's saving grace. This problem is one which the 'symbolic' model of witness seeks to redress.

The term 'symbolic' (as used here) is borrowed from Karl Rahner, and it comprehends witness as wholly exemplifying its object, to the extent that it can point to itself as a manifestation of that object. Further, in Rahner's understanding, the object becomes fully itself only when it has become manifest in its symbol. This concept needs to be explained, and the best place to begin, in order to do this, is with a brief look at Rahner's theology of the Incarnation.

Rahner's theology is transcendental because it begins by identifying the conditions which must have been necessary in order for "the

Word" to have become "flesh" (John 1:14). If the Word became a man, it follows that the capacity for human nature to be assumed by the Word must be a potentiality "objectively identical with the essence of man" [*Rahner, Karl, 'On the Theology of the Incarnation, in A Rahner Reader, ed. Gerald A. McCool, London, Darton, Longman & Todd, 1975, p147*]. For Rahner, this is a proposition which finds support in the fact that it was man that materialised when God spoke into the void; the nature of humanity is thus an anticipation of the Word participating in that nature [*Ibid, p152*]. It is as if humanity is God's chosen 'grammar' within which "the Word can 'express' himself hypostatically" [*Ibid, p145*], and as such, "man is the articulate mystery of God" [*Ibid, p152*]. It is apparent, thus far, that Rahner's understanding of the Incarnation is heavily anthropocentric, however, by attending to his notion of 'symbol', it will become clear how it is possible for Gerald McCool to claim, instead, that Rahner proposes not anthropocentricism, but a "theological anthropology [that] is theocentric and Trinitarian in its focus" [*Ibid, p145*].

For Rahner, a real symbol does not merely represent something, but rather it embodies intrinsically its subject – a subject which only fully becomes itself through its self-expression in its symbol. Karen Kilby points out that Rahner holds this to be true of all reality, for "all being necessarily expresses itself in an 'other', and in fact only fully becomes itself, only 'comes to itself'", in thus expressing itself" [*Karen Kilby, 'Karl Rahner', in Modern Theologians, p100*]. Subsequently, the concept of symbol is the form by which the first and second persons of the Trinity are understood; for the Son is the symbol of the Father, and is thus dependent on the Father, the source and cause of his being. Yet as the Father only fully 'comes to himself' through symbolic expression in the Son, so the Father is distinct from, yet not independent of, the Son [*For Rahner's fuller explanation of this concept see: Rahner, Karl, Theological Investigations, vol. 4: More Recent Writings, London, Darton, Longman & Todd, 1966, pp235-45*]. In this way Rahner's conceptualisation of the Trinity forms the basis for his theology of the Incarnation, to which his anthropology is secondary, as McCool has suggested. Rahner begins with an understanding of 'God in three persons' to explain how it was that the Word became flesh, from which he proceeds to an understanding of human nature that explains how flesh was assumed by the Word.

Rahner's conceptualisation gives full authenticity to the witness of Jesus Christ, for the Word did not somehow use the flesh instrumentally, but became it symbolically, and thus the Word-made-flesh was the true, complete, constant revelation of God. This concept also accredits to some extent the witness of the individual believer, for every human is also a real expression and revelation of God, although fallen and, thus, far from identical to that which he or she reveals [*See: Ibid, p239*]. But Rahner perceives there to be a more faithful witness borne by believers as community. Rahner understands the church to be, quite literally, the Body of Christ; "the symbolic reality of the presence of Christ, of his definite work of salvation in the world" [*Ibid, p241*]. The church's role is to be a continuing symbol of the grace extended in the Incarnation; to express herself in such a way as to be a witness to the saving work of Jesus Christ.

Through Rahner's notion of Symbol, two valuable insights are gained into the character of witness. His insistence on the plurality of believers as the symbol of God recalls the fact that Jesus' declaration in Acts 1:8 ("You will be my witnesses") was given in the plural, and that the object of Christian witness is God in three persons, the God of relationship and of community. This will serve as a useful warning against any model of witness for which an individual is sufficient. Secondly, the totally self-effacing model of witness espoused by O'Donovan is brought into relation with St. Paul's testimony; as Rahner attests that there is a *really* symbolic manifestation of the Creator in his creatures, witnesses must no longer point always beyond themselves, but can in a real sense *be* that to which they bear witness.

Having said this, there is a danger with the optimistic view of the believer expressed in this second point, that the individual seems able to bear witness with a sufficiency that the first point precludes. On the other hand if the church is, as it were, 'sufficiently' "the symbolic reality of the presence of Christ", this idea is hard to reconcile with the knowledge that the church remains, in reality, but a host of sinners, far from the perfection of God who she is said to symbolise. Moreover, if humanity was made to glorify God [*for example, Isaiah 43:7*], then surely it cannot be a sufficient witness that humanity singularly or collectively points to itself.

It is apparent that there needs to be an idea of witness which falls between that which is totally self-effacing, (and thus undermines the realities of Christ's presence in the believer and the church as Christ's body), and that which attributes an unrealistic ability to believers to be a sufficient witness to the perfection of God. This model must avoid exalting the witness to a position which obscures the object of witness, and it must also retain the premise that a community has the potential to bear a more faithful witness than an individual. Nicholas Adams' suggestion that the witness is a "sign" [*Adams, Nicholas, 'Confessing the Faith: Reasoning in Tradition', in The Blackwell Companion to Christian Ethics, eds. Stanley Hauerwas and Samuel Wells, Oxford, Blackwell Publishing, 2004, p209*] will help to articulate how the 'significant' form of witness might fulfil these criteria.

A sign represents its object by virtue of the fact that it embodies that which it signifies as the essence of its own identity. "To witness is not just to say something or show something. It is to become a sign" [*Ibid, p209*], and to become a sign is to become like a word in a language. Continuing this analogy, it can be understood that Jesus Christ, as *the* Word, contains the entirety of the revelation of God within himself. The believer can be but one word, one sign. Nevertheless if that word is rightly spoken and correctly heard, it can articulate truth. In this understanding of the form of witness, three components can be noted. Firstly, the notion expressed by the sign can, and will, express itself (to borrow Rahner's terms) within the grammatical framework of that sign. In other words, it must be the case that God is able and chooses to be witnessed to through his creatures. Secondly, the witness must be capable of faithfully signifying that to which it is a sign. Though humans are irrevocably sinful, they must, in a real sense, be capable of faithfully representing the God to whom they witness, or they are not truly signs, but merely idols. Finally, as Adams notices, "to be a Christian...is to learn how to read the signs of God in the world" [*Ibid, p209*]. The Christian is schooled in a new language which expresses the nature of God and his creation, through which he can converse with God and those who share this language. But it is also the case that "a sign in a language one does not understand does not function as a sign, but as a puzzle" [*Ibid, p209*]. If the sign is to be a witness, it is not enough for the sign to faithfully represent its object. The observer must also be familiar with the rules by which the sign can be read, and so the witness must also be a teacher. The object of witness is not dependent upon the sign for its existence; an object can exist without there being a sign by which it is expressed and / or identified. Yet a sign is dependent upon its object for its existence, for its object determines its nature, its identity and its purpose. Nevertheless, the object must be signified to be communicated. Those who know its name must speak it intelligibly to those who do not. God has ultimately communicated himself in the person of Jesus Christ, but as Jesus prepared to leave this world he tasked his followers with the continuation of this communication, made possible through the Holy Spirit (Acts 1:8).

By this understanding, Christian witnesses can be said to be 'significant' because they must necessarily embody that which they signify. Yet those who come to be able to read these signs will, by the very fact that they *are* signs, be directed beyond them to the object of witness. When witness is understood in this manner, it is also the case that witness will be most fruitful amidst community, where there is dialogue between speakers, listeners, teachers and interpreters. The unique significance of the witness of Jesus Christ was that, in him, an entire language was contained in one Word, but it is the multitude of believers, each individually a sign of God, who comprise the creaturely language of witness.

The Peaceable Model of Witness

Now that some principles of the form of witness have been established, they can be used to evaluate three models of the practise of witness, the first of which is 'peaceable witness'. The command that Jesus gave in the Sermon on the Mount to "settle matters quickly with your adversary" (Matthew: 5:25) is an example of the Biblical precedent to favour peace over conflict and is seen in practice when Jesus was confronted in Gethsemane by the authorities of his time. Peter, overcome by the injustice of the situation, returned the violence of the soldiers (towards his master) with violence, and cut off the ear of the high priest's slave. Jesus, however, responded with an astonishing gesture of peace, and healed the man's injury.

The peaceable witness strives to demonstrate peace by following the example of Jesus not Peter, but it will be shown in this chapter that there are certain interpretations of peace that tend to distort the peace exemplified in the life and work of Christ. The model of peaceable witness comprises instances of Christian witness in which the primary goal is to avoid setting itself up in opposition to the world. When avoidance of conflict is paramount, peace tends to be understood in terms of conformity to, and sympathy with, the world. Three thinkers whose work helps to elaborate such an understanding are Ernst Troeltsch, Paul Althaus, and H. Richard Niebuhr, although for quite different reasons. Before these ideas are considered, however, some initial conceptual analysis of what it means, as a follower of Jesus Christ, to be peaceable, will make it possible, at the end of this chapter, to identify where the faults with this first model of witness lie.

The theme of peace is one that thoroughly permeates Scripture, and the basic premise that the Christian gospel is "the good news of peace through Jesus Christ" (Acts 10:36) should not be denied in any Christian model of witness. Yet it is inevitable that Christian witness will, at some point, meet with some manner of conflict, and so it can be difficult to reconcile the Biblical vision of peace with the present reality of conflict. What then is the Biblical vision of peace, and what is the Biblically peaceable reaction to conflict? In Willard Swartley's study of peace in the New

Testament, he sees that Jesus Christ – according to the words of St. Paul: "he himself is our peace" (Ephesians 2:14) – is the embodiment of peace, and therefore its Biblical definition must be based upon what is revealed in him. Further, the first three gospels seem to relate the idea of peace quite consistently with the themes of the kingdom of God and the gospel, both of which Jesus likewise embodies [*Swartley, Willard M., Covenant of Peace: The Missing Peace in New Testament Theology and Ethics, Cambridge, William B. Eerdmans Publishing Company, 2006, p12*]. Swartley also suggests that the angels' announcement to the shepherds, "and on earth peace" (Luke 2:14), was an indication of what it would be for God's 'kingdom to come' [*Ibid, p11*]. Thus when heaven touches earth, there is peace, and so Jesus Christ, as the physical manifestation of such a meeting, is indeed the peacemaker [*Ibid, p13*].

A definition of peace grounded in Jesus would correspond with the Old Testament understanding of *shalom* as God's will and order for creation, for in Jesus Christ God's plan and purpose for the world are revealed. But it would also denote a peace of forgiveness and love, for peace viewed Christologically is experienced in the gifts of reconciliation and atonement given through Jesus Christ. Because such a definition is grounded in Jesus Christ, not only does it describe the Biblical vision of peace in terms of it being a divine attribute and an eschatological hope, but it also holds a moral claim over all those who desire to be his followers, and live as he lived. Peace in the New Testament is both the peace of God and the peace commanded by God. As Swartley observes, "by stating that the nature of both God and Christ is peace, the ethical mandate to pursue peace finds its strongest theological and incarnational anchor" [*Ibid, p213*].

One definition not found in the New Testament, however, is that which understands peace in terms of security, and which Swartley believes to be widespread in the world today [*Ibid, p1*]. Violence and power are the means by which this kind of peace is attained and maintained, but the gospels clearly state that follow Christ is to accept insecurity (at least by worldly measures), and that violence should not be used to make it otherwise (for example, when Peter draws his sword in Gethsemane). Biblical peace, then, is about bearing witness to the God of peace. It is expressed in love for one's neighbour rather than by seeking of one's own security. It is faithful to the vision of peace that corresponds to God's will for the world, and it practises forgiveness and reconciliation according to the life and work Jesus Christ. Lastly, in the epistles, there is an emphasis on peace within the fellowship of believers as being essential to the good life of that community. Swartley notices that the epistle to the Ephesians consists largely of St. Paul urging the believers to be united in peace, because of the peace they experienced through Christ [*Ibid, p214*]. But further, St. Paul declares that this peace is not only for those who are 'near', but those who are 'far off', and so the community of peace who bear witness to the God of peace are to extend that peace to the rest of the world. With these principles established, this discussion will now turn to the examination of some examples of the peaceable model of witness.

Like Jesus and his disciples, (although in a very different way), theologians in post-Christendom West have found themselves challenged by the authorities of their day. The Christian worldview was contested and, by the time Europe emerged on the other side of the Enlightenment, a drastically different worldview had been established in which Christianity's claim to absolute truth no longer stood. Writing in such a context, Friedrich Schleiermacher has been critiqued for allowing his ideas concerning Christianity to be determined by the world and not by the self-revelation of God [*See: Gerrish, B. A., Continuing the Reformation: Essays on Modern Religious Thought, Chicago, The University of Chicago Press, 1993, pp173-7*] – a charge which makes it possible to identify him as an accessory in Troeltsch's enthusiasm for a 'peaceable' relation to his culture.

The Enlightenments prioritisation of rationalism had universalised the content of religion, and relegated Christ to an archetypal moral figure. Schleiermacher countered such over-intellectualising of Christianity by insisting that the believer's experience of faith, and the particular revelation that came from an encounter with Jesus Christ, was the foundations for a theological system. Kant had rightly insisted that God could not be 'reasoned to', but Schleiermacher wanted to ensure that faith was still considered, even though the object of faith could not be properly known. Consequently, he developed an understanding of faith according to the nature of human consciousness [*Schleiermacher expounds his concept of faith as consciousness in: Schleiermacher, Friedrich, The Christian Faith, eds. H. R. Mackintosh and J. S. Stewart, Edinburgh, T & T Clark, 1999, particularly pp5-25*].

Schleiermacher identified that humans are only *self*-conscious through self-identification in relation to that which is not self; that which is other, and thus humans are intrinsically mutually dependent. Therefore, the experience of faith is the realisation that one is absolutely dependent upon that which is totally 'other' and totally 'independent'. Such a realisation Schleiermacher calls "God-consciousness", which Jesus had to the highest degree, and by virtue of which he was divine [*See: Schleiermacher, Christian Faith, pp385-9*]. By beginning with the experience of the subject, rather than with the object of faith, Schleiermacher runs the risk of falling foul of the Feuerbachian charge that God is merely "the manifested inward nature, the expressed self of a man" [*Feuerbach, Ludwig, The Essence of Christianity, trans. Marian Evans, London,*

Trübner & Co., 1881, p12]. Further, by stressing the contemporaneousness of Christ in terms of his salvific work as redirecting consciousness away from bondage to the sensible and towards God, the importance of the particularity of the historical person of Jesus becomes difficult to defend. Karl Barth realised that this kind of thinking allowed limits imposed by secular culture to moderate how Christianity is to be understood, which is just how Troeltsch deliberately developed his own theology [*See: Gerrish, B. A., 'Friedrich Schleiermacher', in Nineteenth Century Religious Thought in the West, vol.1, eds. Ninian Smart, John Clayton, Steven Katz and Patrick Sherry, Cambridge, Cambridge University Press, 1985, p148, or for Barth's own much longer analysis of Schleiermacher, see: Barth, Karl, Protestant Theology in the Nineteenth Century: Its Background and History, Zürich, SCM Press, 2001, pp411-59*]. Where Schleiermacher, though, with his idea of absolute dependence, never conceded to the concept of the autonomous individual [*Schleiermacher, Christian Faith, pp13-16*], Troeltsch thought this to be the most crucial discovery of the modern world.

Instead of offering a criticism of the de-absolutising of Christian claims, or of the new ontology of human autonomy, Troeltsch was sympathetic to the "new foundations and presuppositions" created by the modern world. He believed that the theologian's task was to "clarify the nature of this transformation" from pre-Reformation ecclesiastical unity to the modern "achievement" of plurality, "and to construct his ethical and religious thought upon it" [*Troeltsch cited in, Chapman, Mark D., Ernst Troeltsch and Liberal Theology: Religion and Cultural Synthesis in Wilhelmine Germany, Oxford, Oxford University Press, 2001, p140*]. Subsequently, as Mark Chapman identifies, Christian ethics for Troeltsch could not be a question of "focusing purely on the moral absolutes of the Sermon on the Mount", but rather it must be "brought into contact with the rough and ready of historical reality" [*Ibid, p142*]. As Schleiermacher had begun with the believer's experience of faith to determine his theology, Troeltsch surveyed history and the behaviour of humanity within it, and based his understanding of the Christian life upon what he found. Where Jesus taught that those who followed him should not be bound by worldly goods, and should readily practise submission, Troeltsch believed that ethics had to respond to the 'facts' revealed by history, such as "the realities of human selfishness and the pursuit of power" [*Ibid, p143*]. Troeltsch so desired to uphold the values he perceived to be "the lasting gains of modernity" [*Ibid, p161*] that he was prepared to compromise the commands of Jesus Christ. When Jesus instructed his disciples to turn the other cheek, he knew that they would follow this ethic of non-retaliation even to their deaths. It seems that Troeltsch also intended to react to the opposition his culture posed to the moral absolutes of the Biblical witness, with a kind of peace. But this peace was struck according to the world's terms.

Where Troeltsch's embrace of the modern world led to a questionable offer of peace, Paul Althaus' objection to it resulted in a dangerously peaceable relationship to the authority of his time. Living amidst the rubble of German Society after the events of the First World War, Althaus watched as modernity (in the form of the Weimar Republic) attempted to build a city from the ruins. Where many identified progress, however, Althaus "recognised in the Weimar only secularism, permissiveness and a breakdown of all moral values" [*Ericksen, Robert P., Theologians Under Hitler; Gerhard Kittel, Paul Althaus, and Emmanuel Hirsch, London, Yale University Press, 1985, p86*]. According to his 'orders of creation theology', Althaus perceived the forms taken by the social life of humanity to be "a human representation of God's order in an imperfect world" [*Ibid, pp100-1*]. Consequently, the order advocated by the Third Reich was theologically appealing to him, and so Robert Ericksen concludes that with the promise of "discipline, reverence for institutions and respect for the churches, he would have thought it absurd not to welcome the National Socialist state" [*Ibid, p86*]. Moreover, Althaus affirmed a Lutheran understanding of Romans 13, holding that secular governments are a necessary part of God's providence, and so should be obeyed [*See: Luther, Martin, 'On Secular Authority', in Luther and Calvin on Secular Authority, ed. and trans. Harro Höpfl, Cambridge, Cambridge University Press, 1999, pp7-9*].

Where Troeltsch was seduced by the 'freedom' in modern ontology, which he believed to be a demythologised form of the freedom espoused in the Christian tradition, [*Chapman, Troeltsch..., p182*] Althaus believed in the power of the *völkisch* notion of a return to pre-modern society in which order and moral law would be maintained [*Ericksen, Theologians..., p85*]. However, in one sense the motives of these two men are alike, for not only did Althaus approve of *völkisch* ideology for its apparent theological value, but also because he agreed with Hitler that "*völkisch* spirit was the spirit of the times and the church must enthusiastically endorse the *Volk* if it were to regain any of its lost impact" [*Ibid, p85*]. Althaus also desired that Christianity might be understood by, and not be in conflict with, the world, and he considered a peaceable relationship between church and state to be a necessary factor in achieving that end.

One last example of the practice of peaceable witness, which contrasts with Troeltsch and Althaus' attempts at 'earthly' peace, is one which recognises the conflict rife in the world, and fixes its eyes on the eschatological realisation of peace. In Helmut Richard Niebuhr's 1932 article, 'The Grace of Doing Nothing', he asserts a particular expression of peaceable witness which appears to have such an eschatological motive at its core. In this article, written reflectively in light of the Sino-Japanese conflict, Niebuhr makes a formal comparison between the response to this disaster by both Christian communities and communist cells. He remarks that both appear inactive because they "see that there is indeed nothing constructive to be done in the present situation, but that, rightly understood, this situation is after all preliminary to a radical change which will eliminate the conditions of which the conflict is a product." [*'Niebuhr, H. Richard, 'The Grace of Doing Nothing', from The Christian Century, 23 March 1932', in From Christ to the World: Introductory Readings in Christian Ethics, ed. Alan Verhey, Cambridge, Wm. B. Eerdmans, 1994, p378*]. However, whereas the communist cells are preparing for immanent change which will enable an outworking of their own ideology, the Christian communities are markedly inactive – believing that the solution they envisage will arrive independent of their own efforts.

A further explanation given for the Christians' inactivity is their recognition of their inability to judge. In response to the faults evident in their present situation, the Christians do not find cause to boast of a superior morality. Instead, they become self-analytical, identifying their own tendency to sin, and practise 'repentance', (understood as preparing to act differently when similar circumstances arise in the future) [*Ibid, p379*]. In this way, they do not call evil good as perhaps Troeltsch and Althaus could be accused of doing, yet they acknowledge that they are not at liberty to judge their neighbour.

Reinhold Niebuhr criticised his brother because he perceived that "the ethical and spiritual note of love and repentance can do no more than qualify the social struggle in history. It will never abolish it." [*'Niebuhr, Reinhold, 'Critique of The Grace', from The Christian Century, 30 March 1932', in From Christ..., pp416*]. Reinhold Niebuhr was wary of 'peace' if it allowed injustice within God's world, for this kind of peaceable witness is not faithful to the God of justice. There is also Scriptural warning against the kind of inactivity which awaits the judgement of God. In Jeremiah, the false prophet Hananiah declares that the Lord will break the yoke of King Nebuchadnezzar from exiled Israel's neck within two years, urging them only to wait upon the Lord for the 'radical change' he will bring (Jeremiah 28:10-11). Jeremiah, however, contends that, on the contrary, the Lord says that they should "build houses and settle down; plant gardens and eat what they produce. Marry and have sons and daughters...Also, seek the peace and prosperity of the city to which I have carried you into exile." (Jeremiah 29:5-7). It seems that, in a time when the people are powerless to change their own political situation, they are nevertheless commanded to be politically involved as citizens in their new home. Moreover, part of this engagement is specifically to seek peace for the city. For both Reinhold Niebuhr and the writer of the book of Jeremiah, it is clear that peace is seen as something to be actively pursued, not passively awaited.

This chapter began by identifying the essential characteristics for a Biblical understanding of peace. Having looked at the ideas which constitute a 'peaceable' model of witness, it is evident that the peace they obtain is lacking in several key components. When Jesus submitted to his enemies he did not do so as a compromise, but in order to overcome them through love. This witness testified to God's order for the world which holds love for others above personal well-being. Troeltsch's idea of peaceableness, however, submitted to the world by denying the absolute goodness of this order proclaimed in Jesus' teachings. Troeltsch and Althaus, by comparison, were concerned that the total otherness of radical Christian witness be adapted in order that it might be more favourable to the surrounding culture. Undoubtedly, Althaus' desire was for a peace that would bring order, but the political system he supported to this end did not bear witness to the order of God who values life and difference. Troeltsch, Althaus and Niebuhr, in different ways, all apparently struggled with the possibility that the radical peace of the kingdom could be made a reality through the church in this aeon, and so the peaceable model of witness seems to lean towards being formally 'self-effacing'. Lastly, it is apparent that, whilst Niebuhr's dormant community would have little opportunity to actively engage with the world, the Christian witness as portrayed by Troeltsch and Althaus loses its 'extraordinariness' and has little resource for practising the kind of radical, even offensive, love exemplified by its object, Jesus Christ.

The Differential Model
of Witness

Whereas peaceable witness attempts to smooth out the creases it finds when the claims of Christianity are opposed to those of the world, the differential model of witness examined in this chapter celebrates that contrast, extolling the unique character of the Christian faith, and refusing to compromise in the face of conflict. This ethos is demonstrated to the superlative degree in the practice of martyrdom, which will therefore provide the focus for this evaluation of differential witness.

Jesus' teaching certainly indicates the possibility and even the inevitability of conflict for the faithful Christian witness. Jesus' instructions in the Sermon on the Mount presuppose that Christians will be the objects of violence (Matthew 5:39), and will be hated, persecuted (Matthew 5:11), and stolen from (Matthew 5:40). Therefore, conflict in itself may be a sign that the Christian is acting rightly. Overwhelmingly, Jesus stresses that conflict in the form of injustice or violence should be endured – but how the Christian should act when he or she sees that injustice is being done to others, or that God's law is being transgressed, is another matter. When Jesus healed a man on the Sabbath (Matthew 11:9-13), and equally, when he prevented the scribes and the Pharisees from stoning the woman caught in adultery (John 8:3-9), he demonstrated the supremacy of God's law summed up in the greatest commandments over any other authority, and would not allow these people to be treated unjustly – even though he knew that his actions would eventually cost him his own life. When Jesus drove the traders from the temple (Luke 19), his protest was that the discrimination being practised in the Father's name bore an untruthful witness to God. Following the example of Christ, or any of the martyrs found in Scripture, it is evident that of paramount concern to them was that their witness remained true and faithful to God, even when it resulted in their deaths. This is highlighted in the fact that the word 'martyr' is derived (in Greek) from the root meaning 'to witness', indicating that the writers of the New Testament saw, as a crucial element of what it meant to bear witness to Jesus Christ, the believer's willingness to die for the integrity of that witness. It should, however, also be remembered that the idea of the 'martyr' is derived from the concept of 'witness', and not the other way around.

One of the earliest and most fervent promoters of martyrdom was Origen. Living in a time when Christians were being persecuted under the reign of Septimius Severus, Origen's own father was killed for the faith he professed, and the young Origen would have followed after him had his mother not restrained him [*See: Wace, Henry, 'Origenes', in The Dictionary of Christian Biography, Literature, Sects, and Doctrines; During the First Eight Centuries, eds. William Smith and Henry Wace, London, John Murray, 1887, p98*]. In Exhortation to Martyrdom, Origen insists that in any situation where a Christian is asked to contravene God's law, where refusal is punishable by death, the believer's only two choices are to be a martyr, or an idolater. He further notices that in Exodus 20, both worship of, and bowing down to, idols are prohibited and, therefore, the Christian must be both inwardly and outwardly faithful to God [*Origen, 'Exhortation to Martyrdom', in The Library of Christian Classics, vol. 2: Alexandrian*

Christianity, trans. and eds. John Ernest Leonard Oulton, and Henry Chadwick, London, SCM Press Ltd., 1954, pp396-7]. This would suggest that not only is God's law a matter of personal purity, but a matter of witness.

Origen goes on to discuss the scriptural example of the witness of the seven brothers in II Maccabees. Origen's account of this incident is strikingly macabre, but it usefully delineates what it is that the martyr's death signifies – so that when the second brother proclaims "you remove us from this present life, but the King of the world shall raise us up to everlasting life" [*Ibid, p409*], this demonstrates both complete trust in the resurrection of Jesus Christ and hope in the eternal life promised to those who believe. When the sixth brother's declaration that "we are paying the penalty of our sins, and are enduring these sufferings willingly" [*Ibid, p409*], affirms that all people are sinners and thus deserve the punishment of death. Finally, the testimony of the last of the brothers to be killed proclaims that God's law is right and just, and must not be compromised or rebelled against: "we obey the law given by God. We must not accept a command contrary to God's words" [*Ibid, p410*].

These four affirmations, (of the realities of the resurrection, eternal life, sin, and the supremacy of God's law), are the substance of this model of witness, and demonstrate why it is regarded by many to be the "perfectly clear witness, without any compromise, to the truth about the good and to the God of Israel" [*Pope John Paul II, 'Veritatis Splendor', in Understanding Veritatis Splendor: The Encyclical Letter of Pope John Paul II on the Church's Moral Teaching, ed. John Wilkins, London, Society for Promoting Christian Knowledge, 1994, p159*]. Indeed, James McClendon understands the witness of the martyr to be one which transcends the God-world distinction that all of the aforementioned models of peaceable witness had to reckon with. In a study of martyrdom within the Anabaptist communities during the period of the Reformation, McClendon presents their witness as both an emphatic submission to the call of discipleship, and a powerful challenge to the beliefs held by the secular authorities who sanctioned their deaths. Therefore "the costly work of the martyr as such *engaged* both believer and culture, both 'Christ' and 'world'" [*McClendon, James Wm. Jr., with Nancey*

Murphy, Witness: Systematic Theology Vol. 3, Nashville, Abingdon Press, 2000, p347]. However, if we examine Origen's ideas in this light, there is a sense in which his understanding of martyrdom seems to be less about witness and more about the introspective spirituality of the individual.

Origen regarded martyrdom as the ultimate test of whether or not the seed of faith in a Christian's life had fallen on "rocky ground or good soil" [*Origen, Exhortation..., p428*], a notion which defines martyrdom as concerning only God and the believer. He further concludes, "For us Jesus laid down his life. Let us therefore lay down ours, I will not say for his sake but for our own" [*Ibid, p422*], thus implying that the martyr does not die for the sake of (or as witness to) the kingdom. He does add that it might also be for the sake of "those who will be edified by our martyrdom" [*Ibid, pp422-3*], which, although making the purpose more public, nevertheless extends its effect only within the community of believers, and not beyond this community into the rest of society. Moreover, it is apparent that there is a danger in the act of self-sacrifice, with its inherent elements of drama and spectacle, of its potential to obscure the purpose for which it is enacted. For a 'perfectly clear witness' to be achieved by the witness who draws so much attention to themselves, witness must be formally conceived 'symbolically' – a concept which this dissertation has suggested to be flawed. Thus Origen's own understanding of martyrdom provides the basis for criticising the propositions that it is a 'perfectly clear witness', and that it 'engages both believer and culture'. John Milbank's article, *The Ethics of Self-Sacrifice* will provide some further reasons why this is so.

The stated task of this article is to invalidate the claim that "the highest imaginable exemplification of the good consists in dying sacrificially on behalf of another or others" [*Milbank, John, 'The Ethics of Self-Sacrifice', in First Things, vol. 91, March 1999, p33*]. Despite there being philosophical and theological agreement upon this point, philosophy must pass through the premise that "self-sacrifice is supremely good only if death is final and unrewarded" [*Ibid, p34*]. This follows from the idea that self-sacrifice must be the purest of gifts in as much as it asks for and receives nothing in return. The consequent problem for Christian theology is that "death in its unmitigated reality permits the ethical, while the notion of resurrection contaminates it with self interest" [*Ibid, p34*]. There is not space here to fully examine Milbank's argument for reasserting resurrection as opposed to death as the necessary foundation for the ethical, and claiming that self-sacrifice is not "most paradigmatic of the good" [*Ibid, p34*], but of particular interest to this discussion is his treatment of 'self'.

Milbank makes three observations that support the hypothesis that martyrdom concerns the self more than the other to whom it is supposed to witness. Firstly, in a somewhat paradoxical sense, for a person to allow themselves to be killed is to take control of the one thing in a person's life which is guaranteed to them, and which nobody can take away from them – their own death [*See: Ibid, p34*]. From this perspective, martyrdom is not a sacrificial 'giving up', but a seizing of power. Secondly, Milbank reveals that self-sacrifice is not the ultimate acknowledgement of the other. For the more "convivial enjoyment" [*Ibid, p35*] is had between persons, the less they project their own subjectivity onto each other, and so it follows that this conviviality between persons is the ultimate way in which they can be mutually acknowledged as individuals [*See: Ibid, pp34-5*]. Thirdly, since this conviviality is inherently reciprocal, both the self and the other are recognised to be "unique and irreplaceable" [*Ibid, p35*]. This reasoning re-establishes the goodness of all creation, and so Milbank concludes, "in order fully to aim for the good, even the sacrificial offering of oneself must sustain the hope of one's own ultimate redemption" [*Ibid, p35*]. Nevertheless, it remains that the mere *possibility* that self-sacrifice might, in some instances, be necessary, indicates an imperfect world, because it necessitates the death of a creature who God has declared to be good.

Further to Milbank's conclusions, it should be noted that in the moment of death, a person is most ultimately an individual. The martyr's death can only ever consist of the witness of one person and therefore falls short of the principle that witness is ideally corporate. Finally, there is one last remark to be made concerning martyrdom's capacity to 'engage' the world. In the twenty-first century West, it has been suggested that there is no overarching "plausibility structure" [*see: Berger, Peter L., The Heretical Imperative: Contemporary Possibilities of Religious Affirmation, London, Collins, 1980, pp26-31*] as can be identified in other cultures, which determines a universal framework within which members of society can make judgements. Instead it is simply up to each individual to choose for themselves. This means that, whilst martyrdom is intended to proclaim an uncompromising commitment to *the* truth, its message will, in fact, not always be heard so unequivocally. There are, after all, many instances of people who have died for causes other than faithfulness to Jesus Christ. Thus whilst there are certainly truths to which martyrdom bears witness, its witness remains incomplete, imperfect and unclear. It runs the risk of being self-promoting, which is incommensurable with witness formally understood as 'significant' as opposed to 'symbolic'. Moreover, it does not bear witness to the good news of life, and life to the full. Lastly, if 'differential witness' in effect lies in distinguishing itself from the world, how can it conduct meaningful dialogue with those who do not already know how to interpret it as a true sign?

A final criticism which is brought against the practice of differential witness and equally the practise of peaceable witness, comes from Bonhoeffer's work. The problem is that in all of the cases examined so far, there is an underlying conception that reality is divided into two spheres, one being of God, and the other of the world. The peaceable models understand there to be a distinction between some kind of 'sacred' and 'secular' authorities. Whilst Christians are under the jurisdiction of the former, it seems that they must also find a way of cohabiting with the latter, whether that be by finding some way to interpret God's law within the boundaries set by 'secular' law (Troeltsch and Althaus), or by resolving to endure worldly life in the faith that at the eschaton a new world under a new authority will emerge (Niebuhr). The model of differential witness holds the same distinction, but posits God's authority in opposition to the worlds, in a conflict which will presumably continue until the eschaton when all authority is brought back under the reign of God – but herein lies the problem.

In juxtaposing different authorities against each other, the authority of Christ is made "partial and provincial" [*Bonhoeffer, Dietrich, Ethics, ed. Eberhard Bethge, London, SCM Press Ltd., 1983, p169*]. To think in terms of two spheres is to suggest that a person might belong to only one of them; but a follower of Jesus Christ, though they live by the spirit, still lives in the world. Similarly, someone who does not follow Jesus Christ, though they live 'by the flesh' still forms a part of God's work of creation and redemption. Though many distinctions are made in the Bible concerning the children of darkness and the children of light, (or the sheep and the goats, or simply the righteous and the wicked), it is not supposed that these peoples form two distinct realms under different authorities, but rather that they are the wheat and chaff of one field. For Bonhoeffer, "the point of departure for Christian ethics is not the reality of one's own self, or the reality of the world; nor is it the reality of standards and values. It is the reality of God as He reveals Himself in Jesus Christ" [*Ibid, p162*]. Bonhoeffer does not allow theologians to deduce a two-sphere reality on experiential grounds. Rather, the starting point must be that through the singular Word all things were made, under the sovereignty of God all things live and die, and by God will all things be judged.

Alan Hirsch understands this to be the claim of the *Shema* (the central prayer and affirmation of Judaism and the declaration of faith in one God). The acclamation that God is one is not primarily descriptive of God's being; rather it poses a radical antithesis to a polytheistic understanding of life. Whenever there is more than one god, life is divided into multiple spheres with each sphere falling under the authority of a particular god. Hirsch believes this to be true not only of Old Testament cultures, but also of the current situation of western Christians where the 'gods' bear names such as "romantic love" and "consumerism" [*Hirsch, Alan, The Forgotten Ways: Reactivating the Missional Church, Grand Rapids, Brazos Press, 2006, p91*]. Christians' acknowledgement that there is one God is synonymous with the confession, 'Jesus is Lord', and thus the *Shema* is "a call to covenant loyalty, rather than being a statement of theological ontology" [*Ibid, p89*].

From this perspective, the apparent gap which the peaceable and differential models of witness (respectively) were so eager to bridge or maintain, is shown to be illusionary. Bonhoeffer insists that "the relation of the Church to the world is determined entirely by the relation of God to the world" [*Bonhoeffer, Ethics..., p176*], and in the modes of that relation expressed in the Incarnation and the cross, the basis for a third conception of witness can be seen. In the Incarnation, the ultimate meeting of 'sacred' and 'secular', God's divinity was not in opposition to his humanity, but the two natures were united in Jesus Christ, unseparated and unmixed. On the cross, he who was without sin became sin. Jesus Christ and the sin he became could not be more diametrically opposed, and yet, in this event, God reconciled the whole world to himself – an action in which the church, as the body of Christ, continuously participates [*See: Ibid, p177*].

The Peaceably Different Model of Witness

It has been suggested that the model of peaceable witness does not take seriously the possibility of a realisation of kingdomly life under the reality of Christ, and differential witness undermines the goodness of life. Peaceable witness tends towards being 'self-effacing' at the expense of the possibility of present transformation, and differential witness runs the risk of positing the individual too highly, obfuscating the object of witness and negating the need for a community. Peaceable witness speaks the language of those to whom it is witnessing, but at the expense of the content of what can only be signified in its own language, and differential witness communicates in a way which only those who have already been taught the signs can understand. There is, however, a third model that Bonhoeffer located in the cross of Jesus, which seeks to reconcile the good (which is to be found in striving for peace) with the refusal to compromise, without allowing what is good to detract from what the witness proclaims about its object. This 'peaceably different' model of witness is also found in Jesus' teaching.

Immediately following Jesus' forewarning to his disciples of their ensuing persecution, he tells them that they are the "salt of the earth" (Matthew 5:13) and the "light of the world" (Matthew 5:14). These metaphors show the disciples how to respond to conflict; how to stand against the pattern of the world and yet be peaceable; how to be peaceably different; how to be Christ's witnesses. Salt and light are harmonious elements in that they have the potential to complement, and enhance, their surroundings. They also connote contrast, irrevocable change, and dissonance. Salt is added to a dish to improve it; it is used in a recipe as part of an overall harmony of ingredients, but it is also utterly different to the other ingredients, and it is precisely because it is harshly different to any other taste that it is a complementary flavour. Likewise, light predominantly has positive connotations and is generally something which is welcomed, but its power is in the fact that it totally opposes darkness; the two cannot be in the same place simultaneously. Salt and light are both totally unique. Each has great strength and goodness in the right context. Each completely negates its opposite – a lit room cannot also at the same time be dark, and a salty dish cannot at the same time be un-salty. Yet both are most desirable when they are diffused amongst that which is different to them – it is not good to eat a whole plate of salt, or stare directly at the sun.

The idea of 'peaceable difference' has been adopted for this dissertation from Milbank, who uses it throughout his work. Milbank conceives of reality in terms of an ontology of 'peaceable difference' [*See: Milbank, John, Theology and Social Theory: Beyond Secular Reason, 2nd Edition, Oxford, Blackwell Publishing, 2006, especially pp429-40*]. This ontology is founded upon a Trinitarian model, understanding that God exists as three distinct persons in perfect unity, and that creation bears the image of such a God [*Ibid, p430*]. Further, Milbank observes that the doctrine of *creation ex nihilo*, in contrast to many other creation accounts which denote some form of dualism, describes a peaceable act for there is no extant thing which is in opposition to that which God creates [*Milbank, John, 'Postmodern Critical Augustinianism: A Short Summa in Forty-Two Responses to Unasked Questions', in Modern Theology, 7/3, April 1991, p229*]. Yet the very process of creating is one of establishing difference [*Milbank, Theology...,* *pp429-30*]. Milbank protests that under a liberal worldview, difference is always negative and so at best can only be tolerated. Given that Catholic Christianity "understands all evil and violence in their negativity to be privation", it also attests to *"the most radical imaginable modern pluralism:* namely that positive differences, insofar as they are all instances of the Good (a condition which of course will never be perfectly fulfilled in fallen time), must for that reason analogically concur in a fashion that exceeds mere liberal agreement to disagree" [*Ibid, pXVI*]. Milbank observes that postmodernism holds an 'ontology of difference', which is taken by many to be an objective descriptive account of the way things are, but he contests that this is but a *'mythos'*, a grand narrative which relies on as many 'non-objective' presuppositions as does any other religious, cultural, scientific or historical account of the world, and he objects that "the postmodern realization that discourses of truth are so many incommensurable language games does not ineluctably impose upon us the conclusion that the ultimate, over-arching game is the play of force, fate and chance" [*Ibid, pp278-9*]. This conclusion, which Milbank identifies to be the neo-Nietzschean view of the history of human life revolving around expressions of the will-to-power, cannot be opposed by the peaceable claims of Christianity because, as Bonhoeffer observed, it is not the case that there is a Godly reality to be pitted against the worldly reality. However, where the narration of the '*mythos*' of postmodernism has come to be the dominant voice within reality, Milbank suggests that the grand story of Christianity, founded on a Trinitarian ontology of peaceable difference, might prove itself capable of out-narrating this understanding of the world.

Whilst Milbank helps to conceptualise the situation in which the Christian witness finds themself, Adams notes that Milbank's theory forms part of that vein of theological writing which is "devoted to showing how Christians should think about doctrine and ethics rather than describing how Christians might enter into debate with other participants in the public sphere" [*Adams, Nicholas, Habermas and Theology, Cambridge, Cambridge University Press, 2006, p11*]. Though Milbank impressively describes the landscape of the Christian who is to live out a peaceably different witness in the world, he does not give instructions as to how exactly the Christian might engage with reality. For this, a final look at the thought of Dietrich Bonhoeffer will provide one possible explanation as to what it is to practise peaceably different witness, and will answer some of the questions to which the solutions proposed by the models of peaceable and differential witness were unsatisfactory. Bonhoeffer often wrote in an impassioned, almost conversational way, stating his theme and then spiralling out away from it in multiple directions towards other related propositions he wished to make. It is therefore difficult to demonstrate succinctly with one example exactly how Bonhoeffer's ideas can contribute to this discussion. The following (somewhat reduced) excerpt, however, from *The Cost of Discipleship*, in which he discusses the 'extraordinary' nature of Christianity, will provide a good starting point:

"What makes the Christian different from other men is the 'peculiar' the [Greek to English transliteration: perisson], the 'extraordinary'...This is the quality whereby the better righteousness exceeds the righteousness of the scribes and the Pharisees...The Christian

cannot live at the World's level, because he must always remember the [perisson].

What is the precise nature of the [perisson]? It is the life described in the beatitudes, the life of the followers of Jesus, the light which lights the world, the city set on a hill, the way of self-renunciation, of utter love, of absolute purity, truthfulness and meekness. It is unreserved love for our enemies, for the unloving and the unloved, love for our religious, political and personal adversaries. In every case it is the love which was fulfilled in the cross of Christ. What is the [perisson]? It is the love of Jesus Christ himself, who went patiently and obediently to the cross – it is in fact the cross itself...

The 'extraordinary' quality is undoubtedly identical with the light which shines before men and for which they glorify the Father which is in heaven. It cannot be hidden under a bushel, it must be seen of men. The community of the followers of Jesus, the community of the better righteousness, is the visible community: it has left the world and society, and counted everything but loss for the cross of Christ.

And how does this quality work out in practice? It must be done like the better righteousness, and done so that all men can see it. It is not strict Puritanism, not some eccentric pattern of Christian living, but simple, unreflecting obedience to the will of Christ...

Hence the ⬚perisson] is the fulfilment of the law, the keeping of the commandments. In Christ crucified and in his people the 'extraordinary' becomes reality." [Bonhoeffer, Dietrich, The Cost of Discipleship, London, SCM Press Ltd., 1996, pp136-8].

Bonhoeffer's ontological understanding that there is only one reality in and through Jesus Christ, enabled him to conceive of the possibility of a peaceable relation between the believer and the world. It has been shown through the examples given in this dissertation that when Christian ethics is grounded upon a two-realities worldview, the central problem is of how there can be a proper relationship between the two spheres. But Bonhoeffer contests that "the New Testament is concerned solely with the manner in which the reality of Christ assumes reality in the present world, which it has already encompassed, seized, and possessed" [*Bonhoeffer,*

Ethics..., p170]. As the above excerpt shows, Bonhoeffer, like Milbank, believed that Christianity assumes reality within the world by its outworking of the better story which it has to offer. This story conflicts in both form and content with the '*mythos*' assumed by postmodernism, but instead of attempting to separate themselves from their culture, the Christian witness must live alongside their neighbours, striving to live out a 'better righteousness'. Elsewhere in *Discipleship*, in an analysis of Matthew 5:13-16, Bonhoeffer observes that salt and light are necessary elements in the makeup of the world [*See: Bonhoeffer, Discipleship..., p104*]. This further suggests that he did not see the Christian witness as something foreign to the world, coming against it in a way that was irreconcilable to it, but rather he saw the people of God as a fundamental *part* of the total reality, living to build God's kingdom and working to establish God's order on earth. Yet even as part of the world, the Christian remains "beyond-all-that" [*Ibid, p137*], living a life which is truly 'extra-ordinary'.

Bonhoeffer goes on in this excerpt to explain how this is practically out-worked: through the most impeccable witness to the teaching and example of Jesus Christ. Counter to the supposition (of those such as Troeltsch) that the absolutes contained in the Sermon on the Mount could not realistically be adhered to, Bonhoeffer believes that only a faithful witness to their instruction could form the content of a life which might out-narrate the world. As he wrote to his brother in 1935: "the restoration of the church will surely come from a sort of new monasticism which has in common with the old only the uncompromising attitude of a life lived according to the Sermon on the Mount in the following of Christ" [*Bonhoeffer, Dietrich, 'Letter from London to Karl-Friedrich Bonhoeffer, January 14th, 1935', in A Testament to Freedom: The Essential Writings of Dietrich Bonhoeffer, New York, Harper San Francisco, 1995, p424*]. Troeltsch had rejected monasticism as that which "aimed to represent the Christian ideal in its purity and which stood in marked contrast with the values of everyday society which were based on natural law" [*Chapman, Troeltsch..., p148*]. Bonhoeffer, though, conversely held that this contrast was the substance of Christian witness; in fact, the 'extraordinary' was for Bonhoeffer the definition of what it "really mean[s] to be a Christian" [*Bonhoeffer, Discipleship..., p136*]. Crucially, instead of advocating the kind of 'monastic' withdrawal which both Niebuhr and Origen advocated in their own way, and which Troeltsch rightly rebuked for its non-engagement with everyday society, Bonhoeffer believed that the 'new-monastic' lifestyle must be lived 'so that all men can see it'.

This text also implies what it might be that Bonhoeffer thought all men would see when they encountered Christians living in this way. Primarily, they would simply see the life of the Christian – which Bonhoeffer sees as identical to 'the light which lights up the world'. Moreover, he sees this light as coming from the Christian community. As Bonhoeffer mentions to his brother, this kind of faithful witness does not restore the individual but the church, and thus he goes on to say, "I believe it is now time to call people *together* to do this" [*Bonhoeffer, Letter..., p424, (emphasis mine)*]. Yet Bonhoeffer is absolutely clear as to the source and purpose of this way of life – it is life lived in imitation of the love of Christ, but more, it is a life that can only be lived because of the love of Christ. When it is lived in this dazzlingly different way, it is done with the sole purpose that men might 'glorify the Father which is in heaven'. The one thing that Bonhoeffer's text does not clearly explain is how the 'language barrier' between the community of believers and the world is to be crossed. Perhaps this is a consequence of his belief that all humanity forms part of the one reality, for if, within that reality, light is universally held to be good, it follows that truly faithful witness will be universally understood as a sign of the good wherever it is seen. Nevertheless, a totally satisfactory account of witness would have to provide some analysis not only of the manner in which the witness speaks, but of the conditions which enable the witness to be heard and understood.

Conclusion

Bonhoeffer's understanding of Christian witness is that it is peaceful, not opposing but out-narrating alternative conceptions of reality. It imitates the peace demonstrated through Christ in that it considers love and forgiveness to be paramount and, because it is founded upon God's greatest commandments, it bears witness to the goodness of God's will for the order of the world. Yet the Christian witness is extraordinary, standing in stark contrast to the way of the world, counting 'everything but loss for the cross of Christ'. In this death-of-self, the witness dies the martyr's death but is born again in Christ – not to live a new 'sacred' life over and against the 'secular', but to celebrate life in the world through the new perspective of seeing all reality under Christ's lordship.

This witness is 'significant'. The community of believers shines like a light before men, which draws those who see it to them, and which signifies its object (who is the true light of the world). Bonhoeffer insists that in the out-working of this peaceably different witness, the witness and the object of witness embody the same message: 'In Christ crucified *and* in his people the 'extraordinary' *becomes reality*'. In fact, the tension inherent in the Christian witness between harmony and dissonance with the world is a reflection of the object of this witness. Jesus Christ, as 'very man' became part of humanity, and to this extent was at peace with the world. But as 'very God', he was utterly different to the world, living a life of perfection alien to all history. Therefore those who live in faithful imitation of Jesus Christ inherently become like the 'salt of the earth' and the 'light of the world', and all that these metaphors imply; they become part of the community of peaceably different witnesses.

If you have found this Study Aid helpful, please leave a review. This will enable other students to find this essay more easily. Thank you.

Bibliography

Adams, Nicholas, 'Confessing the Faith: Reasoning in Tradition' in The Blackwell Companion to Christian Ethics, eds. Stanley Hauerwas and Samuel Wells, Oxford, Blackwell Publishing, 2004, pp209-21.

Adams, Nicholas, Habermas and Theology, Cambridge, Cambridge University Press, 2006.

Barth, Karl, Protestant Theology in the Nineteenth Century: Its Background and History, Zürich, SCM Press, 2001.

Berger, Peter L., The Heretical Imperative: Contemporary Possibilities of Religious Affirmation, London, Collins, 1980.

Bonhoeffer, Dietrich, Ethics, ed. Eberhard Bethge, London, SCM Press Ltd., 1983.

Bonhoeffer, Dietrich, 'Letter from London to Karl-Friedrich Bonhoeffer, January 14th, 1935', in A Testament to Freedom: The Essential Writings of Dietrich Bonhoeffer, New York, Harper San Francisco, 1995, p424.

Bonhoeffer, Dietrich, The Cost of Discipleship, London, SCM Press Ltd., 1996.

Chapman, Mark D., Ernst Troeltsch and Liberal Theology: Religion and Cultural Synthesis in Wilhelmine Germany, Oxford, Oxford University Press, 2001.

Ericksen, Robert P., Theologians Under Hitler; Gerhard Kittel, Paul Althaus, and Emmanuel Hirsch, London, Yale University Press, 1985.

Feuerbach, Ludwig, The Essence of Christianity, trans. Marian Evans, London, Trübner & Co., 1881.

Gerrish, B. A., 'Friedrich Schleiermacher', in Nineteenth Century Religious Thought in the West, vol.1, eds. Ninian Smart, John Clayton, Steven Katz and Patrick Sherry, Cambridge, Cambridge University Press, 1985.

Gerrish, B. A., Continuing the Reformation: Essays on Modern Religious Thought, Chicago, The University of Chicago Press, 1993.

Hirsch, Alan, The Forgotten Ways: Reactivating the Missional Church, Grand Rapids, Brazos Press, 2006.

Kilby, Karen, 'Karl Rahner', in Modern Theologians: An Introduction to Christian Theology Since 1918, 3rd Edition, eds. David Ford and Rachel Muers, Oxford, Blackwell Publishing, 2006, pp92-105.

Luther, Martin, Luther's Works, Vol.25; Lectures on Romans, ed. Hilton C. Oswald, Saint Louis, Concordia Publishing House, 1972.

Luther, Martin, 'On Secular Authority', in Luther and Calvin on Secular Authority, ed. and trans. Harro Höpfl, Cambridge, Cambridge University Press, 1999, pp3-43.

McClendon, James Wm. Jr., with Nancey Murphy, Witness: Systematic Theology Vol. 3, Nashville, Abingdon Press, 2000.

Milbank, John, 'Postmodern Critical Augustinianism: A Short Summa in Forty-Two Responses to Unasked Questions', in Modern Theology, 7/3, April 1991, pp225-37.

Milbank, John, 'The Ethics of Self-Sacrifice', in First Things, vol. 91, March 1999, pp33-8.

Milbank, John, Theology and Social Theory: Beyond Secular Reason, 2nd Edition, Oxford, Blackwell Publishing, 2006.

'Niebuhr, H. Richard, 'The Grace of Doing Nothing', from The Christian Century, 23 March 1932' in From Christ to the World: Introductory Readings in Christian Ethics, ed. Alan Verhey, Cambridge, Wm. B. Eerdmans, 1994, pp378-80.

'Niebuhr, Reinhold, 'Critique of The Grace of Doing Nothing', from The Christian Century, 30 March 1932' in From Christ to the World: Introductory Readings in Christian Ethics, ed. Alan Verhey, Cambridge, Wm. B. Eerdmans, 1994, pp415-17.

O'Donovan, Oliver, Resurrection and Moral Order: An Outline for Evangelical Ethics, Leicester, Inter-Varsity, 1986.

Origen, 'Exhortation to Martyrdom', in The Library of Christian Classics, vol. 2: Alexandrian Christianity, trans. and eds. John Ernest Leonard Oulton, and Henry Chadwick, London, SCM Press Ltd., 1954, pp393-429.

Pope John Paul II, 'Veritatis Splendor', in Understanding Veritatis Splendor: The Encyclical Letter of Pope John Paul II on the Church's Moral Teaching, ed. John Wilkins, London, Society for Promoting Christian Knowledge, 1994, pp77-182.

Rahner, Karl, Theological Investigations, vol. 4: More Recent Writings, London, Darton, Longman & Todd, 1966.

Rahner, Karl, 'On The Theology of The Incarnation', in A Rahner Reader, ed. Gerald A. McCool, London, Darton, Longman & Todd, 1975, pp145-153.

Schleiermacher, Friedrich, The Christian Faith, eds. H. R. Mackintosh and J. S. Stewart, Edinburgh, T & T Clark, 1999.

Swartley, Willard M., Covenant of Peace: The Missing Peace in New Testament Theology and Ethics, Cambridge, William B. Eerdmans Publishing Company, 2006.

Wace, Henry, 'Origenes', in The Dictionary of Christian Biography, Literature, Sects, and Doctrines; During the First Eight Centuries, eds. William Smith and Henry Wace, London, John Murray, 1887, pp96-142.

The Holy Bible: New International Version, London, Sydney, Auckland, Hodder and Stoughton, 1999.

More Parbar Study Aids

The Concepts of Marriage & Divorce in the Hebrew Tradition,
their growth & development to their form at the time of Jesus

David Robertson

This 9,000 word essay was written by the author in 1980 and was subsequently developed into Marriage Restoring Our Vision. It has proved useful to students and to those interested in the Old Testament concepts of marriage and divorce.

The essay is offered to readers and students who wish to study the various biblical texts for themselves and to chart the development of marriage and divorce in the Old Testament.

Also by David Robertson

David Robertson writes both nonfiction and fiction under his own name, and fiction in different genres under the pen names of JB Duncan and Riach Wilson.

He is the vicar of a busy parish in West Yorkshire, England, the son of an internationally known musician, the husband of a wonderful wife and the father of four adult children. Before ordination he worked in a variety of 'ordinary' jobs, some of which sound quite exotic – such as working in a bamboo factory – but the reality was much more mundane (the bamboo factory, for example, manufactured drain rods).

He is interested in most things and enjoys reading and writing in different genres.

Collaborative Ministry
What it is, how it works, & why

Collaborative Ministry is fast becoming a 'buzz phrase' in the church, following on from phrases such as 'every member ministry' and 'the priesthood of all believers'. It is referred to by those who speak and write about leadership, the Church and outreach, but what exactly does it mean? And does it fit with existing leadership structures?

This book comprehensively explores the theology and practice of this style of 'being church', considering the implications for churches both large and small. A central section provides foundational Bible studies, unpacking the themes of authority, acceptance and covenant, while an appendix of group study material offers help for churches considering a collaborative approach.

Marriage; Restoring our Vision

This book aims to restore our vision of God's created purpose for marriage. It allows the Bible to shed light on both our inherited cultural values and our contemporary Christian assumptions. Linking with the vows in the Marriage Service, it examines biblical principles and challenges current practice. The book also unpacks difficult issues such as cohabitation, divorce and remarriage.

Entertaining, thought provoking and stimulating, this book can be read by an individual, used as the basis for a Bible study group or as the foundation for a teaching series. The ideas and images used will communicate clearly to young and old, whether single, married or divorced. For all those wanting to think about the subject, it will help them to discover God's pattern for married life.

What Would Jesus Post?
A biblical approach to online interaction

If Jesus had access to the internet, what would he post? And, as importantly, what wouldn't he post? This book asks intriguing questions of those who engage with the internet; which biblical principles inform its use, and how might Christians steward their online presence?

Through reflecting on online engagement we can establish good principles for online interaction. For adults, children and young people, and ideal for parents, leaders and ministers, home groups and youth pastors.

Fiction ~ David Robertson

KALEB's TESTIMONY

Christian Oblate Zombie Hunters: Book 1

Kaleb is 20, an Oblate of Trinity Cloister, London, and a member of the Watch. His duties are to dispatch the Scourge (the walking-dead), and report on Pestilents (the living-dead). His fear is their 'Judas kiss' by which all flesh is betrayed, so don your armour with prayer, draw your sword, and join him; but be of good comfort: 'Thou shalt be hid from the scourge of the tongue: neither shalt thou be afraid of pestilence when it cometh.' Job 5:21.

Available as eBooks:

BIBLE INSIGHT STORIES

Zack's Difficult Day

Shammai Shares His Supper

Deborah's Denarius

Manny's Missing Mutton

TELL IT AGAIN STORIES

Bertie's Quest for the Perfect Pearl

Fiction ~ JB Duncan

The Holy Rude Diaries combine down-to-earth humour with a hint of the numinous. They are quintessentially British, with British spelling, British idiom and understated British humour - but Glossaries are provided for readers unfamiliar with the terms used.

THE CURATE OF COCKLEIGH

A tale of Anglicans, Angels & Arson

In 1977, Rev John Davidson is the newly ordained Curate of Cockleigh. His ministry is quite ordinary until he meets an anarchist and begins to see angels...

As he navigates his way around mistaken identity, a vindictive detective, a teenager with romance on her mind and a septuagenarian Kung-Fu Rector, his life becomes a frantic rollercoaster ride towards an explosive conclusion.

The Curate of Cockleigh is clever, outrageous, insightful, provocative and very funny.

THE VICAR OF WESTFEIL

A tale of Faith, Farce & Felony

As the millennium approaches and the banks are exploiting the public, St Jude's Church in Westfeil is quietly exploiting the banks. Faced with an enormous repair bill, the Vicar of Westfeil, Rev John Davidson, initiates a scheme that will fund the repairs. The scheme is ingenious, highly successful and has just one, minor problem; it is also completely illegal...

Set against the background of this fund-raising scheme, The Vicar of Westfeil follows the maverick ministry of John Davidson and the fortunes of the people of Westfeil as they move from failure to crowning success.

The Vicar of Westfeil is honest, moving, sly, scurrilous, challenging and, as always, very funny.

THE BISHOP OF BANFORD

A tale of Crosiers, Cherubs & Crime

Maverick vicar, John Davidson, the new Bishop of Banford, is plunged headlong into a diocesan world of relentless work, financial anxiety, repressed sexuality and inspired lunacy. His marriage begins to fall apart, an old flame reignites and unseen enemies move against him. He is forced to consider hard choices – but then he comes to the unwelcome attention of a crime-lord and finally experiences the most terrifying meeting of his life.

The Bishop of Banford is complex, mischievous, astute, compassionate and, of course, very funny.

Amazon Reviews:

'A good read.'

'The Bishop continues to delight us with his heartfelt efforts to do what is right but continues to stumble over his own feet... This third book in the series is also very funny.'

A PAIR OF SHORTS

Two novellas in one volume: *The St Jude's Shuffle* and *Not a* Leg *to Stand On.* Both are available, individually as eBooks but are published in *A Pair of Shorts* in one paperback volume.

THE ST JUDE'S SHUFFLE
A Tale of Decision, Deceit & Dysentery

With clergy interviews, a clandestine fund-raising scheme, a conceited Archdeacon, an uncandid candidate, multiple hidden agendas, devious church members and something nasty lurking in the parish buffet, *The St Jude's Shuffle* follows the fortunes of Westfeil church as they hunt for a new Vicar.

The St Jude's Shuffle is empathetic, honest, intelligent and as readers have come to expect, very funny.

Amazon Reviews:

'Funny, gossipy and true to life.'

NOT A LEG TO STAND ON
A Tale of Pretence, Pride & Paradox

Rev. Canon Austen Pillinger, Bishop's Chaplain, has lost his faith, embezzled diocesan funds and is on the run from a vicious loan-shark. Suicide seems to be his only option until a strange dream promises to change his life forever...

Not A Leg To Stand On is mischievous, intelligent and subtle, and will delight readers who enjoy the piquant taste of black humour.

Available as an eBook

AN APTITUDE FOR AVARICE
A Tale of Perfidy, Posing & Pensions

When antiques dealer Barry Salterton visits a downsizing elderly couple, he cannot believe his luck! Their home is stuffed with treasures and Barry is just the man to take them off their hands. His eye is drawn to a particularly rare and beautiful clock – but as negotiations begin, the deal becomes much less straightforward than Barry hoped...

Fiction ~ Riach Wilson

ABOUT THE SERIES

Every novel in the *Boxed In* series is an independent story in its own right and the series can be read in any order. Each novel is told from the viewpoint of the main character who is, in some way, 'boxed in'. Some characters also appear in other novels – which allows the reader to see them in a different light. Across the *Boxed In* novels and novellas, interconnecting lives build into a fascinating interplay of human choices and intersecting circumstances.

SLINGS & ARROWS

The events of Slings and Arrows take place some three years before Josie Tasker's life is turned upside down by the events in Outrageous Fortune.

She has retreated from paparazzi intrusion and is living a quiet life. She is in her mid-thirties, financially secure, has a wonderful home and good friends – but she reaches a personal crossroads and decides to plunge back into her career. She has the offer of work and romance is in the air – but then a stalker appears and bitter threats overshadow the promise of love.

Can Josie survive these Slings and Arrows?

OUTRAGEOUS FORTUNE

Since fortune first smiled on Josie Tasker, her life as a singer turned actress has become such as dreams are made of. Then she turns forty, and a series of disasters strip Josie of everything.

Does outrageous fortune favour the brave, the rogue or the saint? As Josie negotiates her maze of misfortune she discovers her real friends, a new life and unexpected love.

Outrageous Fortune can be read and enjoyed as an entirely secular, contemporary romance, understood as a very positive journey through loss, or appreciated as an analogy of the well-known Old Testament story on which it is based. However it is read, it is an affirming story of love.

TO THE THIRD GENERATION

Sarah Price is one of life's copers – but when her husband falls in love with another man, her marriage falls apart and so does she. Determined to do her best for her children she seeks help from a counsellor but, as she unravels her past, she uncovers a dark family secret that threatens everything she holds dear.

To the Third Generation, the third novel in the Boxed In series, is poignant, romantic and deeply moving.

SOUL TO SOUL

On what turns out to be an ill-fated business trip, Bella is grateful to find a seat on a crowded train. She is keen to avoid male attention but when she meets an old friend she changes her mind. Although neither of them can remember where they last met, however hard they try, it becomes a chance encounter that changes both of their lives...

Soul to Soul is a novella which can be easily read in one sitting.

TURN AROUND TWICE

Hereseth, a tight-knit fishing community in the Highlands of Scotland, is Ruth's home. New families rarely move in and when the King family arrives, every tongue in the town begins to wag. Ruth, though, is captivated by Marlon...

As she grows up, her future seems secure, but her trials and tribulations demand hard decisions and tough choices. Life can change all too quickly – as Mrs King is wont to say: 'Before you can turn around twice and tap your head.'

Turn Around Twice can be enjoyed as a contemporary romance, appreciated as one woman's journey through the changes and chances of life or understood as a retelling of a widely-loved Old Testament story. However it is read, it is a heart-warming story of hope.

Parbar Publishing

Parbar Publishing is a small, independent publishing company based in the North of England.

Parbar books include:

Adult fiction

Children's fiction

Poetry & Pictures

Christian non-fiction

www.parbarpublishing.com

Facebook

www.ingramcontent.com/pod-product-compliance
Lightning Source LLC
Chambersburg PA
CBHW071829020426
42331CB00007B/1665